Documenting Discipline

Mike Deblieux

American Media Publishing
4900 University Avenue
West Des Moines, Iowa 50266-6769
800-262-2557

Documenting Discipline

Mike Deblieux
Copyright © 1995 by American Media Inc.

This publication is designed to provide accurate and authoritative information in regard to the subject matter covered. It is sold with the understanding that neither the author nor the publisher is engaged in rendering legal, accounting, or other professional service. If legal advice or other expert assistance is required, the services of a competent professional should be sought.

Credits:

American Media Publishing:	Art Bauer
	Todd McDonald
	Leigh Lewis
Project Manager:	Karen Massetti Miller
Editor:	Dave Kirchner
Designer:	Gayle O'Brien

Published by American Media Inc., 4900 University Avenue
West Des Moines, IA 50266-6769
Second Edition

Library of Congress Catalog Card Number 95-75609
Deblieux, Mike
Documenting Discipline

Printed in the United States of America, 1997
ISBN 1-884926-34-7

Introduction

Documenting Discipline shows you how to use progressive discipline as a positive management tool. It shows you how to meet with an employee to help him or her correct a problem. It provides you with a format for writing disciplinary action memos. It focuses on your responsibility as a supervisor to help an employee understand and correct workplace problems.

This book addresses the two types of employee problems—poor performance and rule violations. It shows you how to investigate, approach, and resolve these problems in a positive manner. It also shows you how to document by using the FOSA+ system. FOSA+, facts, objectives, solutions, actions, plus your positive approach to discipline, will help you solve employee problems and protect you and your company from unnecessary legal liability.

Before applying anything you learn in this book, it is important to find out how your organization wants you to handle employee problems. This book gives you a format and an approach. Your company human resources and legal experts can help you apply what you learn within the policy framework of your company and the legal requirements of your state.

As you move forward with the new information you gain from reading this book, remember that the best-kept secret in management is that the way you approach a problem employee determines whether the employee will work to solve the problem or continue on a downhill slide toward termination. If you approach a problem employee in a negative manner, he or she will likely fail. In many cases, you will become involved in a legal review of your actions that will, at the very least, be very uncomfortable. If you approach the problem employee with a constructive and supportive manner, you will significantly increase the chances that the employee will correct the problems you have identified. As a result, you will avoid unnecessary liability for you and your company.

Remember that every employee represents an investment to you and your company. When you add up the cost of hiring, training, and developing an employee, you make a considerable investment in that employee. Before you move to give up on that investment, you should make every effort to assure that you have tried to get the most from it.

Book Objectives

You are most likely reading this book because you want to improve your managerial and supervisory skills. As you begin to invest your time, we think it is important for you to be thinking about what you will gain from this experience. At the beginning of each chapter, we list goals to help you see where you are headed. Here, we would like to help you see what you will gain from reading and applying the entire book.

What You Will Gain

Clearly, the main thing we think you will gain is a new appreciation for your responsibility to carefully and accurately document the steps you take to counsel, coach, and discipline employees. We want you to have an increased awareness of the role you can play in helping an employee be successful. We also want you to be more aware of your role in limiting the legal exposure you and your company can face in dealing with employee problems.

After reading this book and completing the exercises it contains, you should be able to:

◆ Collect accurate facts to use in making decisions about performance and rule-violation problems.

◆ Set specific objectives to show an employee how to correct a problem.

◆ Offer solutions to help an employee find a way to reach your objectives.

◆ Clearly inform an employee of the action you will take if the problem is not corrected.

You may have some additional goals of your own. Take a minute to list them below.

_____

_____

_____

_____

_____

About the Author

Mike Deblieux is a nationally recognized human resources management trainer and consultant. He is president of Mike Deblieux Human Resources in Tustin, California. He designs and presents training programs on human resources-related issues such as Documenting Discipline, Writing Performance Reviews, Interviewing, Preventing Sexual Harassment, and Equal Employment Opportunity. He presents over 100 programs each year to a variety of private, public, regional, state, and local organizations.

Mike provides a full range of HR consulting services to small- and medium-sized companies. He writes and updates employee handbooks and personnel policy manuals.

Mike is an instructor for the University of California, Irvine Extension Human Resources Management Certificate Program. The Extension honored him with the 1991 Distinguished Instructor Award.

Mike is a Course Leader for the American Management Association (AMA), The Employers Group, and the Professionals in Human Resources Association (PIHRA).

Mike has also written *Legal Issues for Managers: Essential Skills for Avoiding Your Day in Court* and *Stopping Sexual Harassment Before It Starts: A Business and Legal Perspective* for American Media Publishing. American Media Inc. has produced two training videos based on Mike's books: *How to Legally Document Employee Discipline* and *Legal Issues for Managers.* The books and videos may be ordered by calling American Media Inc. at 800-262-2557. Mike can be reached by phone at 714-669-0309 or by e-mail at mdhr@aol.com.

Acknowledgments

The author wishes to thank Art Bauer, Todd McDonald, and Leigh Lewis at American Media for their help, support, and assistance on this book. Special thanks and appreciation is also extended to Lee Paterson, Attorney at Law, for his role as an encouraging mentor.

Table of Contents

Chapter *One*

Getting Started

Chapter Objectives

▶ Explain the two main uses of the FOSA+ system.

▶ Describe two reasons for writing and retaining effective documentation.

▶ Explain your role as a supervisor in addressing employee-performance or rule-violation problems.

▶ Approach common employee problems from an objective perspective.

The FOSA+ System

D ocumenting discipline is one of the most important supervisory tasks you will ever undertake. With properly written documentation, you increase the chances that an employee will correct a work-related problem. When that happens, you both should be congratulated and move on to even greater challenges.

Documenting discipline is one of the most important supervisory tasks you will ever undertake.

If the problem continues, however, you must be able to show that you made a reasonable effort to work with the employee to resolve the problem. When prepared correctly, your documentation will demonstrate your efforts and significantly reduce legal liability for you and your organization.

FOSA+ is an acronym for the steps you need to take to write an effective disciplinary action memo to an employee who is performing poorly or who has violated company rules. These steps will help you define the problem and explain what must be done to correct it.

1

FOSA+ also can serve as an agenda to follow when you meet with an employee to discuss performance or rule-violation issues. It will help you plan for the meeting and stay focused on the issues you need to address in the meeting.

FOSA+ stands for:

F   Facts to define the problem.

O   Objectives that explain to the employee how to resolve the problem.

S   Solutions that can help the employee reach the objectives.

A   Actions you will take if the problem is not corrected.

+   Plus your overall efforts to help the employee succeed.

After you've read this book, completed the exercises it contains, and applied what you've learned, you should be able to address employee-performance and rule-violation problems effectively.

Why Is Documentation So Important?

Not so very long ago, supervisors handled most disciplinary issues simply by talking to the problem employee. They resorted to writing things down only when the problem was very serious. In those days, most employees felt powerless to challenge any actions taken by their supervisors.

In the 1960s, a variety of federal and state personnel-related laws were passed, and employees began to use these laws to challenge disciplinary actions by filing lawsuits. When these cases went to trial, both the employee and the supervisor attempted to explain what happened. When clear documentation was not provided, juries were more sympathetic to the employees. In cases where the supervisor was able to provide clear documentation, the courts and the juries considered the supervisor's story more carefully. As a result, employers learned that good documentation is a critical part of an effective defense against employee lawsuits.

In addition to its legal importance, effective documentation is important for at least three other reasons. First, it helps an employee understand your concerns and shows the employee what to do to resolve the problem. Second, it helps you be more objective and fair by forcing you to read and reconsider your own reasons for taking disciplinary action. Third, it helps ensure that all supervisors are consistent in dealing with employees by providing a document for human resources, senior management, or legal counsel to review before any disciplinary action is taken.

Take a Moment

Yes No

☐ ☐ Are your disciplinary actions designed to help employees succeed?

☐ ☐ Do you document discipline in a clear, concise, timely manner?

☐ ☐ Do you ask your senior manager or an experienced human resources person to review your disciplinary actions before you present them to an employee?

☐ ☐ Do you always give an employee a chance to explain his or her side of a story or problem before you decide what to do?

If you answered "no" to any of these questions, use the space below to jot down steps you might take to improve.

_____

_____

_____

Why Do We Use Discipline?

Supervisors sometimes are reluctant to use discipline to correct employee problems. Typical reasons include:

- ■ I don't want to hurt the employee's feelings.

- ■ Maybe if I'm patient, the employee will figure it out without me getting involved.

- ■ No matter what I do, the employee is going to get defensive and argue with me.

- ■ You can't fire anybody around here anyway.

These concerns can be legitimate. But they grow out of a misunderstanding of what discipline is all about. The word *discipline* means "to train (a person) to act according to the expected norm." Although discipline also can be punitive (as in the case of a termination), in most cases it should be taken as an effort to help an employee resolve a problem and become successful in the job.

> The word *discipline* means "to train (a person) to act according to the expected norm."

Take a Moment

Look up the verb *discipline* in your dictionary. Write the definitions you find in the space below.

_____

_____

_____

_____

If you use discipline only to punish an employee, you very likely will make the problem worse and create unnecessary liability for yourself and your company. You should use discipline as a positive training tool to help the employee succeed. Only if the employee does not succeed should you be prepared to take further disciplinary action, up to and including termination.

The Supervisor's Job in Documenting Discipline

Today's most effective supervisors are first and foremost trainers and coaches. The work performed in most organizations requires people to work together to solve problems. It requires them to be creative and innovative. And it often requires a high level of customer service. Employees look to their supervisors to help them perform these complex and difficult tasks successfully.

When things go well, the job of a supervisor can be satisfying, rewarding, and challenging. But when an employee doesn't perform properly, it's your responsibility to try to help the employee resolve the problem and succeed in the job. If the problem is corrected, you should congratulate the employee and yourself for having grown from the experience. But if the problem persists, you must be sure that you have been a supportive coach, followed your company's procedures, and clearly documented your actions.

Helpful Hint

Never attempt to deal with an employee problem when you are upset or angry. Take the time to distance yourself from the problem and relax. Ask yourself how you would like your supervisor to handle the problem if you were the employee. Be sure to approach the employee with a positive, constructive attitude. Never lecture. Ask questions to find out what the employee knows or does not know. Do your best to teach the employee and coach him or her to be successful.

Common Situations

As a supervisor, you are called upon to address a variety of employee-performance and rule violation problems. Each situation is unique. You must proceed cautiously, checking and double-checking your information before you decide what to do. Regardless of the problem, you must approach it in a way that demonstrates that you are trying to help the employee succeed. In order to limit potential liability for yourself and your company, always consult with your human relations or legal staff before you decide what to do.

Some of the most common problems you will face and the key issues you must consider are discussed on the following pages. In each case, a sample FOSA+ disciplinary action memo shows how the problem and the resulting actions might be documented.

Poor Attendance

A late or absent employee creates problems for supervisors, coworkers, and customers. When you deal with an attendance problem, you also must decide whether the employee is entitled to certain rights under the Americans with Disabilities Act and the Family and Medical Leave Act.

Actions

When you address attendance issues, you must:

◆ Follow your company's attendance policy.

◆ Be consistent in the way you apply the policy to all employees.

◆ Investigate to be sure you have a complete and accurate explanation of the employee's attendance.

◆ Carefully consider extenuating circumstances.

◆ Review the situation with your senior manager or a human resources representative before deciding what action, if any, to take.

1

> **Regardless of the problem, you must approach it in a way that demonstrates that you're trying to help the employee succeed.**

Sample FOSA+ Memo: Poor Attendance

February 10, 1997
To: Bruce Black
From: Danielle Deblieux, Manager
RE: Oral Warning

On December 7, 14, and 21, you were absent from work. Company Rule 9 states: "Employees will be disciplined for excessive absenteeism." Each of these absences was on a day before your scheduled day off. On December 27, I counseled you about your attendance on the job. You were absent again on January 5 and 16. On January 29, I again counseled you about your attendance on the job and cautioned you that further absences would lead to formal disciplinary action. On February 1, you called in sick. This was the day before your weekend off. When you returned to work on February 4, you told Bob Barrette, Supervisor, that you had gone dirt-bike riding in the desert. On February 7, I met with you to discuss your attendance. During this meeting, I gave you an oral warning about your attendance.

I want to be sure you understand that I am seriously concerned about your attendance record. I expect you to be at work, on time, every day you are scheduled to work unless you have a bona fide medical emergency that prevents you from coming to work or are authorized in advance to take time off. If you are unable to come to work, you must contact me, Sam Jones, or Jorge Rodriguez in advance. If you miss work for medical reasons, you must submit a doctor's note indicating that you are medically able to return to work before you may begin working.

If you are having medical problems, you should use the company medical plan. If you want to use some of your accumulated vacation days for time off, you should submit a request at least two days in advance.

A copy of this memo documenting your oral warning will be placed in your file. Unless you follow this directive, you will be subject to further serious disciplinary action.

I have received a copy of this memo:

_____
Bruce Black/Date

Poor Performance

When a job is done incorrectly, time and resources are lost. As a supervisor, it is your job to help employees perform at their best. Good performance requires that you communicate about performance standards on a regular, ongoing basis. Employees perform at their best when they are properly trained and work in an environment in which they are encouraged to grow and develop.

When you write and conduct employee performance reviews, you are communicating about performance. Make sure that you conduct your reviews on time, that they are accurate and factual, and that they are in writing so the employee can use the information to perform the job more effectively in the future.

Actions

When you address a performance problem, you must:

◆ Be sure you have provided the appropriate and necessary training for the employee to do the job.

◆ Be sure you have provided the proper tools and resources for the employee to perform the work.

◆ Be sure that you have provided clear and complete instructions for the project or work assignment.

◆ Investigate to be sure you have a complete and accurate explanation of the employee's behavior.

◆ Review the situation with your senior manager or a human resources representative before deciding what action, if any, to take.

Sample FOSA+ Memo: Poor Performance

May 31, 1997
To: Jose Rodriguez, Sales Executive
From: Nicole Deblieux, Sales Manager
RE: Written Warning–Work Performance

On February 10, I gave you an oral warning about your failure to meet your sales goals. Between January 5 and February 5, you sold $10,000. Your goal during that period was $20,000. I told you that, during the period from February 11 through May 15, I expected you to sell at least $100,000. I also told you that if you did not meet this sales goal, you would be subject to further disciplinary action, up to and including termination. I provided you with a cellular phone and arranged for you to attend a sales-association meeting that included several workshops on improving sales volume.

Between February 11 and May 15, you sold $30,000. On May 25, you told me your cellular phone did not work for the first week and that it kept you from meeting your goal. You told me you were averaging 18 calls or visits to customers each week. I explained that you were the first sales executive in the company to have a cellular phone and that you were the only salesperson below your sales quotas. Your sales quotas are the same as for other sales executives.

Your sales goal for the next 60 days is $120,000. You must meet this goal. You must increase client contacts from your current average of 18 per week to at least 30 per week. Your cellular phone now is fully operational. I expect you to use it between site visits to make calls to current or potential customers.

There is a time-management workshop for sales executives on June 10. I suggest you attend. You should pay particular attention to the information on organizing your work.

This written warning will be placed in your personnel file. If you do not meet the sales goal established for you for the next 60 days, I will take further disciplinary action, up to and including termination.

I have received a copy of this memo:

_____

Jose Rodriguez/Date

Attitude Problems

One of the most difficult challenges you will ever face as a supervisor is an employee with a bad attitude. An employee who does not get along with others, or one who is rude or difficult to communicate with, can have a negative effect on the morale of an entire work group.

You need to approach attitude problems very carefully. If you tell someone he or she has a "bad attitude," you are almost sure to make the problem worse. You must approach an attitude problem on a job-related basis. In other words, you need to identify how the attitude manifests itself on the job. You need to talk more about what the employee does than why he or she does it. For example, if an employee does not like dealing with customers—but still does it in a friendly, courteous, helpful manner—he or she very likely is performing the job effectively. You may not be able to change an employee's attitude, but you can insist that he or she perform the job to your objective performance standards.

Actions

When you address an attitude problem, you must:

◆ Identify the job-related performance problem the attitude is creating.

◆ Evaluate possible work-related causes of the attitude problem, including your own supervisory style.

◆ Investigate to be sure you have a complete and accurate explanation of the employee's behavior.

◆ Focus on the behavior, not the person, in order to resolve the problem.

◆ Review the situation with your senior manager or a human resources representative before deciding what action, if any, to take.

> **You may not be able to change an employee's attitude, but you can insist that he or she perform the job to your objective performance standards.**

Sample FOSA+ Memo: Attitude Problems

January 9, 1997
To: J. T. Chipshoulder, Customer Service Representative
From: Molly Deblieux, Customer Service Manager
RE: Written Warning—Work Performance

You joined our company on November 1. You attended two weeks of customer service training during your first month. The training program emphasizes the importance of working with our customers to meet their needs. Several of the exercises involved role-playing to show you how to work with customers under various conditions. You worked beside Brent Villalobos, Senior Customer Service Representative, to learn from him during your first two weeks in the department.

Yesterday, when you were assisting a customer, I walked into the showroom and heard you say, "I am sick of listening to you complain about our products. Did you ever think it doesn't work because you are dumb?" When I asked the customer what had happened, she said she had asked several questions about the Owner's Manual. She said you were impatient and rude. She said that you had talked loudly to her, almost shouting. When I asked you what had happened, you told me, "I am tired of dealing with customers who are too lazy to read the manual."

Your behavior yesterday was unacceptable. Your primary job is to help customers. When you talk to customers, I expect you to listen carefully to their comments. I expect you to confirm what the customer says by using statements such as, "I believe you are asking...," or "That is a good question. Let's look in the manual for the answer." When you have a problem communicating with a customer, I expect you to ask another Customer Service Representative to help you.

The Training Department is offering a new course on stress management. If you would like to take the course, please see Pat Smith to sign up for it.

This is a written warning. It will be placed in your personnel file. You must meet or exceed the objectives outlined in the third paragraph. If you do not meet or exceed them, you will be subject to disciplinary action, up to and including termination.

I have received a copy of this memo:

_____

J. T. Chipshoulder/Date

Rule Violations

Most companies have a list of work rules that employees are expected to follow—rules that prohibit serious acts or actions such as drug or alcohol use on the property, theft, unsafe work practices, or violence.

In addition to company rules, you also may have departmental or work-unit rules that employees are expected to follow. As a supervisor, you are responsible for telling your employees about these rules so that they can understand and apply them. You also should remind all of your employees about these rules on a regular and ongoing basis.

Actions

When you address a rule-violation problem, you must:

- Be sure that the rule says what you think it says.

- Be sure that the employee knew or should have known that the rule existed.

- Investigate to be sure that you have a complete and accurate explanation of the employee's behavior.

- Be sure that the rule has been enforced consistently with other employees, both within and outside your department.

- Review the situation with your senior manager or a human resources representative before deciding what action, if any, to take.

> As a supervisor, you are responsible for telling your employees about these rules so that they can understand and apply them.

Sample FOSA+ Memo: Rule Violations

February 28, 1997
To: Irving Schultz, Warehouse Worker
From: Ron Vasquez, Warehouse Manager
RE: Suspension Notice

On December 27, I gave you a written warning because of your conduct at the company Christmas Party. At the party, I saw you grabbing female employees and kissing them, even though they told you to stop it. Your behavior was a violation of our sexual harassment policy. The written warning cautioned you that any future violations of the policy would result in severe discipline.

On February 24, you worked late with Sylvia Porter. On February 25, she reported that you had asked her to go to bed with you. As part of our investigation, I asked you for your version. You denied that any incident had occurred and suggested that she was out to get you. Two days later, I confronted you with a witness. You admitted that you had suggested to Sylvia that she have sex with you.

You must follow the company's sexual harassment policy. A copy of the policy is attached. You must avoid verbal, physical, and visual behavior that may be offensive to others. Other than shaking hands, I expect you to avoid touching other employees. I expect you to avoid unwelcome personal contact with other employees, including requesting dates or making suggestive comments. I expect you to attend the Sexual Harassment seminar that is scheduled for next Thursday in the training room. I expect you to write a report explaining what you learned in the workshop and to meet with me on Monday at 9:00 a.m. to discuss your report.

If you have any questions about conduct in the workplace, I suggest that you see me or M. J. Smith in Human Resources before engaging in it.

Your actions are in violation of strict company rules. I am suspending you without pay from March 1 through March 5. If you engage in any further violations of this rule, you will be terminated immediately.

I have received a copy of this memo:

_____

Irving Schultz/Date

As you continue reading this book, you will learn more about how to address these and other employee problems. Although each situation is unique to the people involved, the checklists and sample memos you have just read will give you a place to start your analysis of the problem you are addressing.

Take a Moment

Make a list of the last three employee problems you have addressed; at your next opportunity, review the documentation you kept to determine how you might improve it:

1. _____

2. _____

3. _____

Self-Check: Chapter 1 Review

Now that you've read Chapter 1, use this space to review what you've learned. If you aren't sure of an answer, just refer to the text. Suggested answers appear on page 82.

1. What are the two things you can do with the FOSA+ system?

   a. _____

   b. _____

2. There are at least four reasons for preparing effective disciplinary-action documentation. What are they?

   a. _____

   b. _____

   c. _____

   d. _____

3. What does the word *discipline* mean?

   _____

   _____

4. First and foremost, supervisors today are:

   a. _____

   b. _____

5. Regardless of the situation you are addressing, the two steps you must always take are:

   a. _____

   b. _____

Chapter *Two*

Your Incidents Diary

Chapter Objectives

▶ Plan and create an effective incidents diary.

▶ Develop a habit of writing down important employee events, including instances of both effective and ineffective performance.

▶ Use your incidents diary to write effective disciplinary documentation.

Planning Your Incidents Diary

Your incidents diary should be accessible and up-to-date.

Keeping an incidents diary is a habit you must develop and practice. It involves writing down significant events that occur with each of your direct reports. Significant events are things such as:

◆ Conversations about work assignments.

◆ Informal counseling or coaching sessions.

◆ "Good work!" kudos.

◆ Customer complaints and compliments.

◆ Disciplinary actions.

Most supervisors keep their incidents diary in their calendar. Some keep it in a computer file. Others keep it in a paper file folder. Wherever you keep it, your incidents diary should be accessible and up-to-date. Keep it in whatever place and format will let you use it on a regular basis.

2

Helpful Hint

Your incidents diary is your record of key events that relate to a particular employee. Keep in mind, however, that the reason you make entries is because you want the employee to succeed in his or her job. Don't keep secret notes. If something is important enough to write down, it's important enough to discuss with the employee. Whenever you take the time to make an entry in your incidents diary, make sure you also take the time to discuss the incident with the employee.

You need to create an easy-to-use system that you will use consistently. Your system should clearly identify the event (it should detail the who, what, when, where, and why). Carefully review the examples that follow. Notice that the diary entries are short and to the point. They provide just enough information to refresh your memory—but not so much that you'll put off making an entry whenever a significant event occurs.

Take a Moment

Where is the best place to keep your incidents diary?

_____

_____

Why?

_____

_____

Sample Incidents Diary

Monday, January 15   **Sample Counseling Note**

9:00 a.m. *Mary was 15 minutes late this morning. Asked her why. She said it was because she had child-care problems. She agreed to work until 5:15 tonight. Told me she hoped to have a new day care center by the end of the week.*

Tuesday, February 3   **Sample Oral-Warning Note**

3:30 p.m. *Gave John an oral warning because he was not wearing his safety glasses when operating the glazer. He attended safety class last week. Summarized oral warning in memo. John refused to sign. Hue witnessed his refusal to sign. Gave John a copy; sent copy to Personnel.*

Wednesday, March 21   **Sample Oral-Warning Note**

4:30 p.m. *Placed Juan on a one-day positive-discipline leave. Told him to consider whether he wants to keep working here and to return with a memo explaining what he can and will do to complete his work on time. Gave him a copy of the memo and placed copy in his file. He signed the original.*

Friday, April 5   **Sample Oral-Warning Note**

9:00 a.m. *Mrs. Gonzalez called to say that Hue had been particularly helpful handling her complaint about our products. She said Hue was courteous and prompt. I told Hue about the compliment and wrote her a note thanking her for being especially supportive with our customers.*

An incidents diary is a reminder of an event—a memory-jogger. At the very least, it can tell you what happened and when. If an employee's behavior deteriorates, your incidents diary can serve as a record of what you did to try to help the employee resolve the problem. The notes in your diary can help you write clear and effective counseling memos, performance evaluations, and warning memos.

2

What Should You Record?

Recording positive performance will help you write effective reviews. Your incidents diary should record the following types of events.

Positive Performance

You should note whenever an employee meets or exceeds a significant performance expectation. Your notes will let you give the employee specific examples of successful performance. For example:

> Recording positive performance will help you write effective reviews.

- January 15: Jones & Company called. Said Bill saved an order for us through after-sale follow-up. Thanked Bill for a good job.

Take a Moment
Practice making an entry in your incidents diary about the positive work performance of an employee.

Date:_____

Employee:_____

Incident:_____

Performance Objectives

You should note in your incidents diary whenever you explain an important job, work assignment, or responsibility to an employee. Your note should indicate that, on a certain date, you explained a performance objective or a set of objectives for the employee to meet. For example:

Note all instances of employee training.

■ February 20: Met with Kay. Explained the company procedures for cash control. Told her she must follow those procedures.

Training

You also should note all instances of employee training, both personal instruction and on-the-job training. Your notes should record the subject of the training and the name of the person who conducted it.

■ September 28: Showed J. V. how to operate drill press. Made K. L. available to answer further questions.

Take a Moment

Practice making an entry in your incidents diary about the training an employee has received.

Date:_____

Employee:_____

Incident:_____

Investigations

When you investigate a minor incident, you should add a note to your incidents diary to help you remember who you talked to and what was said. (For major events, of course, you also will need to write a memo to explain your findings.) For example:

■ February 29: Asked Mary if she knew who took the crane out of the yard. She said she saw Alison Owen drive away in it at 7:00 a.m.

Counseling

You should note all instances of employee counseling as they occur. Even though the counseling may be informal, it demonstrates that you're working with the employee to resolve a problem in its early stages. If the employee doesn't resolve the problem, it may be important to demonstrate that you began working with him or her as soon as you became aware of the problem. If you don't make notes at the time you offer counseling, it will be difficult, if not impossible, to reconstruct the dates and times later. For example:

■ March 3: Joan late 10 minutes. Reminded her of company attendance policy. She said she would be on time from now on.

Progressive Discipline

You should note each step of progressive discipline (oral warning, written warning, last-step option, and termination) in your incidents diary. Even though these actions also will be documented in memos or letters, it's important to note them in your incidents diary so your records are complete. For example:

■ July 5: Suspended Jack for three days for taking company property home without permission.

> **You should note each step of progressive discipline in your incidents diary.**

Keeping Your Documentation

Your incidents diary is an ongoing, up-to-date record of your efforts to help your employees succeed. If an employee ultimately is unsuccessful in his or her job, your incidents diary will help show that you did your job as an effective supervisor.

In the event of a lawsuit, your decision to discipline or terminate an employee may not come before a judge or jury for three to five years. This means you must write down all important events and store your notes in a safe place. Many termination lawsuits are lost because the supervisor could not find the necessary documentation and, therefore, was unable to prove that an employee violated a rule or performed poorly. In the courtroom, it's essential that you have accurate and complete documentation to support your decisions. If you can't support your testimony with clear, accurate documentation, your company and, quite possibly, you personally could face significant attorney, court, and settlement costs.

Self-Check: Chapter 2 Review

Now that you've read Chapter 2, use this space to review what you've learned. If you aren't sure of an answer, just refer to the text. Suggested answers appear on page 83.

2

1. What is the purpose of an incidents diary? (Circle one)

   a. To build a case to fire an employee.

   b. To keep track of incidents as they occur so you won't get sued.

   c. To keep track of incidents as they occur so positive and critical employee documentation is factual and accurate.

2. True or False?
   You don't need to talk to an employee about the issues you note in your incidents diary.

3. Where is the best place to keep an incidents diary?

   _____

   _____

4. What kinds of notes should you keep in your incidents diary?

   _____

   _____

Chapter *Three*

Finding the Facts

Chapter Objectives

▶ Identify facts using the five Ws.

▶ Identify facts using your five senses.

▶ Understand the difference between a subjective statement and a factual statement.

▶ Gather factual information from third-party witnesses.

Using the FOSA+ System

You should always follow a planned format when you document employee discipline.

Y ou should always follow a planned format when you document employee discipline. A planned format will help you cover all of the necessary points. It will also help you analyze your actions before you take them to be sure you have carefully considered the many variables involved in progressive discipline.

As we saw in Chapter 1, FOSA+ is an acronym for a system that can help you plan your documentation. FOSA+ stands for Facts, Objectives, Solutions, and Action. The "+" is a reminder that you must approach the problem with the goal of creating an opportunity for the employee to succeed.

When you use FOSA+ as your outline to write a disciplinary action memo or document, you will always be following a consistent format. You will clearly explain to the employee what he or she has done wrong. You will establish specific objectives for the employee to meet in order to resolve the problem, and you will show that you are working to be a supportive coach. Most importantly, you willl be documenting that you have placed the employee on notice, that the problem is serious, and that, if not corrected, it will place his or her job in jeopardy.

FOSA+ Step 1: Facts

Facts are the keys to effective documentation. Facts include the five Ws:

◆ **What** happened

◆ **When** it happened

◆ **Where** it happened

◆ **Who** was involved

◆ **Why** it happened

When you describe a situation with facts, you leave out your own conclusions, opinions, and emotions. For example, here is a description of a work project that is based on conclusions:

■ Your report was late. It was the worst report I've read in years. It left out all the important information. There was no way I could release it to the Board of Directors.

Now, let's describe the same report using facts:

■ Your report was due January 11. On January 10, you assured me you were almost done writing it. I received your report on January 14. When I asked you why it was late, you told me, "Deadlines are so artificial. What's a day here or there?"

When I read the report, I found seven misspelled words. The pages were numbered 1, 2, 3, 7, 9, and 12. The report did not have an executive summary, as required by our Board of Directors report format. It also did not include a financial analysis. My December 12 memo to you states, "The board report must include a detailed financial analysis."

Notice how both paragraphs are free of emotions or conclusions. Notice also that, when you read this summary, the facts allow you to conclude that the employee has failed to prepare a professional report.

Describing a situation with facts gives the employee, your manager, and any outside reviewer a clear picture of why you are concerned about the employee's behavior. It allows you to objectively document that the employee has not performed at the expected level.

Take a Moment

Describe your work area using only facts.

The wall in front of me is (color)

_____

My desk has (#) _____ stacks of paper on it.

The picture on the wall shows a (thing)

_____

_____

We naturally tend to describe situations with subjective thoughts, assumptions, and conclusions. You're making a subjective statement when you say things like:

■ He was drunk.

■ She was sick again.

■ He has a bad attitude.

These statements actually are conclusions. When you hear a conclusion, you almost automatically question it. For example:

3

■ How do you know he was drunk?

■ When was she sick before?

■ What do you mean by "a bad attitude"?

Facts, on the other hand, are much easier to accept and verify. For example:

■ Two people reported that his breath smelled of bourbon.

■ She was out sick Thursday, Friday, and again today.

■ He said, "Stick it in your ear."

Using Your Five Senses

To successfully document employee behavior, you must describe your direct observations of the employee's behavior or record the direct observations of others. An excellent way to limit yourself to facts when you describe a situation is to focus on using your five senses:

◆ I saw . . .

◆ I heard . . .

◆ I touched . . .

◆ I smelled . . .

◆ I tasted . . .

These statements are factual. They simply report your observations. If your statements are factual, they probably will support your conclusions. For example:

■ John, I saw you report to your work station at 8:10 a.m. You are scheduled to report to work at 8:00. I heard you tell Jane Smith that you overslept because your alarm clock didn't go off.

When you read this statement, you conclude that the employee was ten minutes late because he failed to check his alarm clock.

On the next page are examples of factual statements that can help you properly document employee behavior.

> **An excellent way to limit yourself to facts when you describe a situation is to focus on using your five senses.**

Conclusion	Fact
You were late.	I saw you report to your desk at 8:35 a.m. (Sight)
You are a thief.	I heard you tell Fred that you took the money. (Hearing)
You didn't clean the walls.	When I ran my hands over the walls, I could feel the oil. (Touch)
The linens were not washed correctly.	When I smelled the new laundry, it smelled sour. (Smell)
You were drinking on the job.	I saw you drink from the glass on your desk. When I tasted the liquid in it, it tasted like vodka. (Taste)

3

Take a Moment

Think about an instance of employee discipline that you've addressed in the past. List three facts about the situation based on using your senses.

1._____

2._____

3._____

Subjective Statements

Sometimes you will need to make a subjective statement in order to prove a point. When you do use subjective statements, make sure you support them with facts. For example:

Subjective Statement	Factual Statement
You are hostile.	On February 1, March 3, and March 28, you used the words "damn you" and "go to hell" to other employees in front of customers. When I discussed this with you on March 29, you told me that it was none of my business and that I had no right to tell you what words to use. Your hostility toward customers and management (subjective) is not acceptable behavior in this company.
You were drunk.	You were under the influence of alcohol (subjective). Your speech was slurred, your eyes were bloodshot, and your breath smelled strongly of liquor.
You are a poor salesperson.	You are performing poorly (subjective). In March, you sold $500,000. Your volume was 40 percent below department average and 25 percent below minimum standard. In January, we agreed that your goal for the first six months of the year would be $5,000,000. You are now 90 percent behind your goal.

Third-Party Observations

Third parties often are good sources of important facts. In fact, sometimes they can be even more credible than an employee or a supervisor. If there was another observer to an employee incident, you should try to get a signed statement from the person. If that is not practical, ask a trusted witness to be present in the room when the third party explains what he or she knows about the incident. Whenever another person describes an employee's behavior, you should ask questions to help the person focus on factual, objective descriptions of what they saw, heard, felt, tasted, or touched.

When you report the observations of others, you also must be careful to describe those observations in factual terms. For example:

■ They told me they saw you . . .

■ He said he heard you . . .

■ He said he tasted . . .

■ She said she smelled . . .

■ They both said they could feel the dirt on the surface . . .

Consider the case of the supervisor who was told that an employee was dealing drugs on the job. The employee who came forward with this information happened to be the supervisor's oldest and most valued friend. The supervisor acted on the information and fired the accused employee. The ex-employee sued. When the case came to trial and the supervisor asked his friend to testify, she refused, explaining that she feared her family would be attacked by drug dealers. She told the supervisor that if she were called to testify, she would deny everything.

The supervisor was left out on a limb by himself, with the ex-employee sawing off the branch. Before taking any action, the supervisor should have obtained a written statement from his friend detailing everything she knew. He also should have tried to get statements from other employees. If he had documented his information before taking action, he could have avoided this problem.

Sample Third-Party Statement

November 21, 1997
Los Angeles

My name is Brenda Cordray. My home address is 254 McMillan Avenue, Ramona, California. My phone number is 619/555-6513.

On Monday, November 20, 1996, at about 10:00 a.m., I was standing in the coffee room. I was facing the north door to the room. The door was closed. Ted Jones came into the room. He was holding a financial calculator in his right hand. It was brown and looked just like the company calculator that I have on my desk.

I saw him hand the calculator to George Danchuck, the Office Assistant. George took the calculator from Ted and placed it in a plain cardboard box that was sitting on the floor.

I then left the coffee room.

I have reviewed this statement on the date indicated below and swear to the best of my recollection under penalty of perjury that it is true.

_____   _____
Brenda Cordray, Assistant Vice President   Date

In addition to witness statements, you also should collect any other pertinent reports or records that exist. For example, accident reports, police reports, computer records, time cards, and other such material all might help you document what happened. You also should ask yourself whether you need to document the location of the incident with photographs, videotapes, or drawings.

Third-Party Statement Case Study

Let's look at the facts in part of a sample written warning given to an employee with an attendance problem.

3

```
February 15, 1997
To: Bruce Black
From: Danielle Deblieux, Manager

RE: Written Warning

On February 10, I gave you an oral
warning because you were absent from work
on December 7, 14, and 21; January 5 and
16; and February 1. Each absence was on a
day before your scheduled day off. I
explained to you that you are expected to
be at work and ready to work by 8:00 a.m.
each day you are scheduled, unless you
are medically unable to report to work or
are scheduled in advance to be off. I
told you that you are required to bring a
note signed by a physician for any future
absence. I also told you that additional
unexcused absences would lead to further
disciplinary action.

Yesterday, February 14, you called in
sick. When you returned to work this
morning, you had no excuse for your
absence. I asked you for a note from a
physician. You told me you did not have a
note and that you did not want to get
one. Company Rule 9 states:  "Repeated
unexcused absences or a pattern of
unexcused absences is grounds for
discipline."
```

When you include old facts in your documentation, you help the reader understand why you have become concerned enough to take the next step of progressive discipline.

The sample memo to Bruce Black cites two types of facts: old facts and new facts. Notice how the first paragraph describes events that have taken place some time ago. These are old facts. The second paragraph lists the most recent events leading to up the written warning. These are new facts. When you include old facts in your documentation, you help the reader understand why you have become concerned enough to take the next step of progressive discipline.

Self-Check: Chapter 3 Review

Now that you've read Chapter 3, use this space to review what you've learned. If you aren't sure of an answer, just refer to the text. Suggested answers appear on page 83.

1. Why are facts the keys to effective documentation?

   _____

   _____

2. Create your own facts and rewrite this subjective statement to make it a factual statement.

   ■ You answered the phone incorrectly.

   _____

   _____

   _____

3. True or False?
   Third-party statements do not have to be signed.

4. You should include both old facts and new facts in a warning memo because: (Circle one)

   a. You don't want to leave anything out.

   b. They provide a more complete explanation of why you are taking a particular action.

   c. They help prove that the employee was wrong and should be disciplined.

Chapter *Four*

Objectives, Solutions, and Actions

Chapter Objectives

▶ Explain what the employee must do to be successful (objectives).

▶ Add a coaching element to your memo to help the employee meet your objectives (solutions).

▶ Communicate what will happen if the employee does not meet your objectives (actions).

FOSA+ Step 2: Objectives

The second step in the FOSA+ system—objectives—involves telling the employee what he or she must do to resolve the problems you have identified with facts. It is often a good idea to involve the employee in deciding what needs to be done. However, as a supervisor, you are ultimately responsible to decide what the employee must do to meet or exceed your expectations.

Supervisors frequently assume that employees know, or should know, what to do on the job.

Supervisors frequently assume that employees know, or should know what to do on the job. This assumption often leads to problems. Unless you can demonstrate that you told an employee what you expect, you cannot hold him or her responsible for failing to meet those expectations. Thus, if you want your disciplinary action to be successful, you must be able to document that the employee knew exactly what you wanted him or her to do to resolve the problem. Remember to make a note in your incidents diary each time you talk to an employee about job performance or company rules.

Setting Performance Objectives

When you set performance objectives, you must either:

◆ Give the employee a specific behavior pattern to follow.

or

◆ Set a specific result for the employee to achieve.

For example:

■ You must turn your computer on, call up the word-processing program, and type the memo exactly as it is written (specific behavior).

■ You must sell five copy machines per month (specific result).

4

When you define a specific behavior or result, you establish a method of measuring the employee's performance. An employee can use subjective (nonmeasurable) objectives as an excuse for poor performance.

In one case, for example, a supervisor told an employee he had been late six times in the previous month and to "improve your attendance." The following month, the employee was late five days. The supervisor terminated him for being late 11 times in a two-month period. The employee defended himself by saying that he had improved in the second month. Clearly, the employee was trying to take advantage of the supervisor's subjective statement. But the supervisor erred in giving him the opportunity. The supervisor should have said, "I expect you to be at work on time and ready to work each day you are scheduled to work."

When you define a specific behavior or result, you establish a method of measuring the employee's performance.

When you write an objective, you must be sure it is:

◆ Specific

◆ Positive

◆ Required

◆ Complete

A *specific objective* clearly defines the task the employee must accomplish or the result he or she must achieve. For example:

Incorrect
- Do a better job with customers next time.
  (This is a very general objective. You can't measure it.)

Correct
- Greet each customer with a smile. Always start the conversation by saying, "Good morning (afternoon, evening). My name is Elizabeth Lamoine. How may I help you?"

Incorrect
- Clean this area up.

Correct
- You must organize the storage room by Friday. Place the boxes and heavy items on the bottom shelves. Place the paper, toner, file folders, and other frequently used supplies on the shelves near the door. Label each shelf to show what it contains.

Take a Moment

Write a specific objective that tells an employee about one of your expectations.

_____

_____

_____

_____

A *positively worded objective* tells the employee exactly what to do. For example:

Incorrect

■ Don't forget to wear your safety glasses next time.
(This is a negatively worded objective. It tells the employee what not to do.)

Correct

■ The company safety rule requires you to wear safety glasses at all times in the plant. I expect you to put your safety glasses on before you enter the manufacturing area.

Incorrect

■ Don't come to another meeting unprepared.

Correct

■ You must prepare for meetings. That means reading the materials that are given to you before the meeting, making notes on them, and writing out your questions or ideas for discussion. If you are making a presentation, you must prepare handouts and overhead slides to help participants follow you.

4

Take a Moment

Write a positively worded objective that tells an employee about one of your expectations.

_____

_____

_____

_____

A *required objective* makes clear that the employee must do what you are telling him or her to do. For example:

Incorrect
- It would be helpful if you would check your work.
(This statement allows the employee to decide whether or not to check the work. If the employee doesn't check his or her work, you can't hold him or her accountable.)

Correct
- You must check your work before you turn it in. Your base numbers must be correct. Your math must be computed correctly.

Incorrect
- Try to get the report done by Thursday.

Correct
- Your final-draft report must be turned in to me by Friday. It must be free of typographical errors and formatted according to the example on page 56 of the procedure manual.

Take a Moment

Write a required objective that tells an employee about one of your expectations.

_____

_____

_____

_____

A *complete objective* considers variables and alternatives that may affect an employee's ability to do the job properly. If you provide an incomplete objective, you may give the employee a convenient excuse for not completing the work. For example:

Incorrect

■ Take care of everything for me.

Correct

■ You must complete your analysis of the computer project by January 9. Your report must evaluate the equipment available from at least four vendors. I expect you to work with Claire Chesick, Purchasing Manager, to contact computer vendors. If you have difficulty identifying qualified vendors or are unable to perform any part of this analysis, I expect you to discuss the problem with me before December 21.

4

Take a Moment

Write a complete objective that tells an employee about one of your expectations.

_____

_____

_____

_____

● Objectives, Solutions, and Actions

Here are several examples of performance objectives to help you write a required objective that is specific and positively worded.

Issue	Documentation
Attendance	In the future, I expect you to be at work and ready to begin working at 8:00 a.m. each day you are scheduled to work.
Honesty	When I ask you for information about company business, I expect you to tell me what you know at the time I ask for the information.
Deadlines	In the future, I expect you to complete your monthly status report in time to be typed, proofread, and corrected by the first of each month.
Reports	Your reports must include an analysis of the customer's equipment problems, the reasons for the breakdowns, the steps you have taken to correct the problems, and your recommendations for future action.
Communication	In the future, I expect you to tell me when the computer is down. I expect you tell me about the problem within one-half hour of the time you become aware of it. If I am not available, I expect you to tell Bob Andreini or Lauren Griffith.
Quality	Your reject rate must be reduced to less than ten parts per 1,000 by January 10 and to less than five parts per 1,000 by March 1.
Cleanliness	You must maintain a clean work environment. This means that you must clean up any liquid or powder spills immediately and that you must sweep your work-area floor at the beginning of your shift and between 1:00 p.m. and 2:00 p.m. each day.

In Chapter 3, we used a fictitious employee, Bruce Black, to give you examples of facts (page 41). Let's continue the memo to Bruce with a paragraph on objectives.

■ Bruce, I expect you to be at work, on time, every day you are scheduled to work unless you have a bona fide medical emergency that prevents you from coming to work or are authorized in advance to take time off. If you need to miss work, you must call me directly. If I am not available, you must speak to Sam Jones or Jorge Rodriguez. If you do miss work, you must bring a physician's note that indicates you are medically able to return to work. Unless you have a note, you will not be permitted to begin working.

Note how Danielle (Bruce's supervisor) has included a statement to tell Bruce what to do if she is not available (to call Sam or Jorge). This statement makes her objective complete.

4

FOSA+ Step 3: Solutions

The third step in the FOSA+ system is to offer solutions that, if used, will help the employee meet the objectives you have established. Offering an employee solutions to help him or her resolve a problem is one of the most important steps you can take. A solution demonstrates that you offered help to change the employee's behavior and that you are acting as a coach to help him or her succeed in the job. Documenting that you gave the employee solutions will increase your credibility with your manager and outside reviewers such as judges, juries, and administrative agency investigators.

> Offering an employee solutions to help him or her resolve a problem is one of the most important steps you can take.

The solutions you offer don't have to be elaborate. For example, if you have an employee who has problems performing the job, you might suggest that the employee take a related course or workshop. If you have an employee who has violated a rule, you could suggest that he or she reread the rule and then ask follow-up questions to verify that the employee understands it.

Here are a few examples of solutions that you could include in your disciplinary documentation.

Issue	Documentation
Coaching	I will work with you on the next project to help you learn how to do it.
Training	I suggest you take an accounting course at a local college.
Resource Person	If you have questions about the documents assigned to you, you may ask Joan to help you or to review your work before you turn it in.
Resource Materials	I'm sending you a book that explains our spreadsheet software. The index provides a quick reference for finding answers to questions you might have about building financial models.

A solution is an option. That is, unlike an objective, it's not something absolutely required of an employee. It's simply your suggestion of a way the employee could meet or exceed your objective. For example, if an employee were struggling with a new word-processing program, you might consider solutions such as:

■ I have a book in my office library that's written for new users of this word-processing program. If you'd like to borrow it, please ask J. T. to get it for you.

■ The community college offers a course called *Word-Processing Applications for Business.* If you're interested in this or other courses, you should check with Human Resources to see if they are covered by tuition reimbursement.

■ J. T. used our new word-processing program in a previous job. Feel free to ask her for advice or help if you run into difficulties with the program.

In Chapter 3, we used a fictitious employee, Bruce Black, to give you examples of facts (page 41). Let's continue the memo to Bruce with a paragraph on solutions.

■ Bruce, you are covered by the company health plan. It covers the majority of costs for treatment after you meet your deductible. It may help if you take advantage of this benefit.

4

FOSA+ Step 4: Action

The fourth step in the FOSA+ system is to document the action you intend to take if the employee does not meet your objectives. If an incident is serious enough to bring to an employee's attention, you must make sure you communicate:

1. The specific action you are taking now (for example, an oral warning or a written warning).

2. The action you will take if the employee's behavior falls short of your objectives.

An action is critical because it communicates the seriousness of the situation and your commitment to seeing the employee resolve the problem.

For example, if you are counseling the employee, you must explain that you are counseling the employee and that you'll meet with him or her again to discuss performance. On the other hand, if you will giving an employee a warning notice, then you must explain that he or she is receiving a warning notice and that if the problem is not corrected, it will lead to further disciplinary action, up to and including termination.

An action is critical because it communicates the seriousness of the situation and your commitment to seeing the employee resolve the problem. It also tells the employee that his or her job is in jeopardy.

On the next page are some sample actions to consider.

Issue	Documentation
Training	I will follow up next week to see if you're applying the information from the training class.
Counseling	I will meet with you in 30 days to see if your attendance has improved.
Written Warning	I am giving you a written warning that will be placed in your personnel file. If you do not meet the objectives I have outlined, you will be subject to further disciplinary action, up to and including termination.
Last-Step Option	You will be suspended for three days without pay beginning Tuesday, May 12. If you do not meet the objectives I have outlined above, you will be subject to further disciplinary action, up to and including termination.
Termination	You are terminated effective immediately.

4

Using our fictitious employee, Bruce Black, let's continue the memo to Bruce with a paragraph on actions.

■ This written warning will be placed in your personnel file. If you do not meet the attendance objectives I have outlined in this memo, you will be subject to further disciplinary action, up to and including termination.

The entire memo to Bruce Black is shown on the next page.

February 15, 1997
To: Bruce Black
From: Danielle Deblieux, Manager
RE: Written Warning

On February 10, I gave you an oral warning because you were absent from work on December 7, 14, and 21; January 5 and 16; and February 1. Each absence was on a day before your day off. I explained that you are expected to be at work and ready to work by 8:00 a.m. each day you are scheduled, unless you are medically unable to report to work or are scheduled in advance to be off. I told you that you are required to bring a note signed by a physician for any future absence and that additional unexcused absences will lead to further disciplinary action.

Yesterday, February 14, you called in sick. When you returned to work this morning, you had no excuse for your absence. When I asked you for a note from a physician, you told me you did not have a note and that you did not want to get one. Company Rule 9 states: "Repeated unexcused absences or a pattern of unexcused absences is grounds for discipline."

Bruce, I expect you to be at work, on time, every day you are scheduled to work unless you have a bona fide medical emergency that prevents you from coming to work or are authorized in advance to take time off. If you must miss work, you must call me directly. If I am not available, you must speak to Sam Jones or Jorge Rodriguez. If you do miss work, you must bring a physician's note that indicates you are medically able to return to work. Unless you have a note, you will not be permitted to begin working.

Bruce, you are covered by the company health plan. It covers the majority of costs for treatment after you meet your deductible. It may help if you take advantage of this benefit.

This written warning will be placed in your personnel file. If you do not meet the attendance objectives I have outlined in this memo, you will be subject to further disciplinary action, up to and including termination.

I have received a copy of this memo:

FOSA+ Step 5: Plus

The plus in the FOSA+ system represents your overall approach to addressing employee-performance and rule-violation issues. In too many cases, discipline is used just to "get rid of" an employee. But if applied properly, discipline can communicate to the employee the need to change. And it can demonstrate that the company has been fair to the employee in its efforts to correct employee problems.

As explained in Chapter 1, a supervisor is both a trainer and a coach. A good trainer helps people learn. A good coach ensures that every member of the team understands and is able to carry out his or her role to help the team succeed. When you use the FOSA+ system successfully, you're making every effort to create opportunities for the employee to succeed. If, in the end, the employee fails, it will have been in spite of your best efforts to help him/her succeed.

4

Self-Check: Chapter 4 Review

Now that you've read Chapter 4, use this space to review what you've learned. If you're not sure of an answer, just refer to the text. Suggested answers appear on page 84.

1. When you set an objective, you must either:

   a._____

   b._____

2. List the four key characteristics of an objective:

   a._____

   b._____

   c._____

   d._____

3. Use a job you're familiar with to rewrite this objective so it includes the four characteristics you listed above.

   ■ You need to do a better job next time. Don't forget to check your work. I would really appreciate it if you would work hard at this. Most importantly, do the best you can in the future.

   _____

   _____

   _____

4. Why is a solution important?

_____

_____

5. Is this statement a solution or an objective?

■ In the future, you must greet customers by smiling and saying, "Good morning (afternoon or evening). Thank you for visiting our store. How may I help you?"

6. What is the purpose of an action?

_____

_____

_____

4

7. The plus in the FOSA+ system is there to remind you to take a positive approach to discipline. It reinforces an expectation by employees and the courts that you use progressive discipline to create an opportunity for the employee to succeed. The plus is important because: (Circle one)

   a. It is impossible to terminate employees today.

   b. Employees, the law, and the courts look to supervisors to provide leadership. Good leaders set the example and work to help their people understand their roles and responsibilities.

   c. The courts have made things so complicated that managers have to play a game to win lawsuits.

Chapter *Five*

Progressive Discipline

Chapter Objectives

▶ Describe the basic steps of progressive discipline.

▶ Discuss valid reasons for terminating an employee.

Progressive Discipline

In today's legal environment, you must be able to show that you took a rational, systematic approach to addressing an employee problem. It's not good enough to "build a file on an employee." You must demonstrate, with credible documentation, that you made a sincere effort to help the employee resolve the problem.

You must demonstrate that you made a sincere effort to help the employee resolve the problem.

Progressive discipline is a six-step system that courts, administrative agencies, and juries expect supervisors to follow. The six steps are:

◆ Training

◆ Counseling

◆ Oral warning

◆ Written warning

◆ Last-step option

◆ Termination

When you use progressive discipline, you are demonstrating that you're making a reasonable effort to create an opportunity for the employee to succeed.

In some cases, you don't need to include every step of the process. If an employee makes a major mistake or commits a serious rule violation, you might skip most of the six steps. For example, if an employee embezzles several thousand dollars from the company, you would move directly to termination. On the other hand, for a 20-year employee with an attendance problem, you might give several counseling sessions before taking any formal disciplinary action. The same employee might receive several oral and written warnings prior to termination. Below is chart showing how progressive discipline is designed to work.

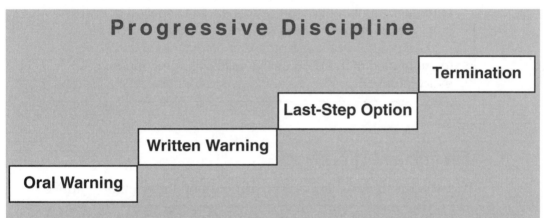

Progressive Discipline

Termination

Last-Step Option

Written Warning

Oral Warning

Formal Actions: The steps shown above the Consequence Line are formal disciplinary actions. You must talk with the employee, make notes in your incidents diary, and write memos explaining the disciplinary actions you've taken. The employee must receive copies of the memos, and copies must be placed in the employee's personnel file.

CONSEQUENCE LINE*

Informal Actions: The two steps below the Consequence Line are informal. There is no threat to the employee's job or job security. But you still must talk to the employee and make a note in your incidents diary.

Counseling	Training

* Your goal above and below the Consequence Line is to create an opportunity for the employee to succeed. The consequence of failure below the line is informal action. The consequence above the line is formal disciplinary action, up to and including termination. When you use the steps above the line, you must tell the employee in writing that his or her job is in jeopardy.

5

Helpful Hint

Companies establish their own progressive-discipline procedures. Check with your human resources representative to be sure that you understand the procedure your company follows.

In some companies, the procedure is not spelled out in the employee handbook. Instead, the handbook explains that the company reserves the right to take disciplinary action if and when it deems it to be appropriate. This gives the company additional flexibility in deciding how to handle a particular situation. When the procedure is spelled out in an employee handbook, there's the possibility that it can be misinterpreted as a guarantee that employees are entitled to every step of the progressive-discipline procedure in every situation.

Termination Notice

If you want to avoid unnecessary litigation, a termination notice can be the most important document you ever write. In most terminations, the employee is told orally about the termination. In other cases, the employee actually is given the notorious "pink slip." However, only rarely is the employee given a statement of the reasons for the termination.

When an employee takes a complaint to an administrative agency or an attorney, the agency or attorney usually will ask why the employee believes he or she was fired. When the employee has been given a termination notice stating the facts behind the decision, the administrative agency or attorney must read and consider the document. If the employee can't effectively refute the facts in the document, the case will end then and there without any further involvement by the company. But if the employee doesn't have a clearly written termination notice, he or she is free to indulge in fantasies about what occurred. You and your company then are in a position of having to defend against the employee's recollection of the incidents that led up to the termination.

Reasons for Discipline

Not long ago, employers could terminate an employee for practically any reason. Two events have significantly eroded this wide-ranging discretion. First, there has been a dramatic increase in protective legislation. Within the last 30 years in the United States, there have been hundreds of state and federal laws enacted that include antidiscriminatory protection for employees. In less than a generation, this country has enacted more laws to protect employee rights than exist in any other country in the world. Today, there are few, if any, employees who can not claim membership in one or more protected classifications. Almost any terminated employee can allege some discriminatory reason for his or her discharge.

Second, in the United States, it was always assumed that an employee had the right to quit his or her job for any reason and that the company had an equal right to terminate the employee for any lawful reason (at-will employment). In other words, if an employee went to work for a company and did not get along with his or her manager or was not as productive as the company demanded, the employee could quit or the company could terminate the person. That concept has been eroded so badly that any employer who fires someone for "incompatibility" or "personal conflicts" is almost guaranteed a lawsuit.

An employer could still fire someone for a subjective reason and win a lawsuit, but the cost might not be worth the victory. At a seminar on employee documentation, a company president once told how he had fired an employee for "incompatibility" and won the case. When asked what it cost him to "win" the case, he stated, "Five years in the court system and over $400,000 in legal fees." He could have "won" for a lot less time and money if he had just identified an objective reason for disciplining the employee and then documented the case.

5

Objective Reasons

Most discipline and termination litigation occurs when an employer can't demonstrate objective reasons for the action. Juries rarely are willing to let an employee lose a job because of a personality conflict with the boss. In many cases, they conclude that there is a personality problem but that the supervisor is the one with the problem. An employer who wants to discipline an employee without risk of litigation has to document a valid, objective reason for the termination.

There are three valid, objective reasons for terminating an employee, but only two of them are grounds for discipline.

1. Reduction in Force

An employee can be terminated whenever there has been a change in the technology of the job, when the job no longer exists, or when the job has been combined so that another employee can perform it. Some companies call this a reduction in force, others a layoff. Since this is not a disciplinary action, the employer has only to show that there was some legitimate change in the business and that there were objective criteria for the process through which the laid-off employees were selected.

In the last ten years in the United States, hundreds of thousands of employees have been laid off on both short-term and permanent bases. In the lawsuits that have resulted from those reductions, the courts have demanded two types of documentation:

1. Documentation that explains the business reason for the reduction.

2. Documentation that shows objectivity was used in selecting employees to be laid off.

Courts and administrative agencies have given wide latitude to employers to make business decisions to change, shut down, or reduce their operations. Reductions in sales, technological changes, and relocations of facilities all have been approved by the courts as legitimate reasons for a layoff. However, in these cases, the companies still had to provide documentation to show that the reason for the layoff was legitimate. Before selecting employees for layoff, a company should collect and store documentation that supports its business reasons for the layoff.

The major pitfall for employers engaged in a layoff is the choice of selection criteria. Companies may not use obviously discriminating reasons such as age, sex, or race to decide who will be laid off. However, other criteria may be equally unlawful. Courts have held that rate of pay, pension eligibility, and reverse seniority (longest service first) also are discriminatory criteria and cannot be used. Valid criteria for layoff selection are performance, productivity, prior discipline, seniority, and future need. When all the employees in a unit are being laid off, the valid selection criteria is lack of work. Before laying off employees, companies must document that they are using consistent selection criteria and that the employees selected all meet those criteria.

> **Documentation is doubly critical in the instance of a single-person layoff.**

Documentation is doubly critical in the instance of a single-person layoff. Courts are suspicious of single-position layoffs because they often are used to hide a termination for work performance reasons. When only one employee is being laid off, the company should carefully review its documentation before taking action.

2. Violation of Company Rules

Violation of company rules and policies is a valid, objective reason for employee discipline. Tardiness, absenteeism, theft, falsification of company records, and sexual harassment are all examples of valid, objective reasons for termination.

In one case, a company was considering the termination of a manager for poor performance. Among other things, the manager had taken several hundred dollars worth of liquor that was left over from a company reception. This was not a performance problem but, in fact, a violation of the company rule against theft. After considering the whole case, the company successfully terminated the employee for theft and ignored the rest of his performance problems.

Take a Moment

Most companies have a list of work rules defining the major offenses that will lead to discipline or termination. It's important for you to know these rules. Where do you keep your copy of them? When was the last time you read them?

You should also remind your employees about these rules from time to time. You can do this by posting them on a bulletin board, talking about them in employee meetings, or writing about them in your company newsletter.

3. Inability or Failure to Perform

An employee's inability to perform the work or negligence in performing the job is the third valid, objective reason for discipline. If an employer can document a decline in performance or can show that the employee's performance does not meet a reasonable, objective standard, then the employer can discipline and, if necessary, terminate the employee.

In another case, a supervisor wanted to terminate an employee for poor performance. A review of the case showed that the supervisor charged the employee with achieving a specific production goal but that the employee kept falling short. The supervisor was convinced that the employee was capable of meeting the goal but purposely was not trying hard enough. She wanted to terminate him for "not trying hard enough." Unfortunately, she had no documentation to demonstrate that the employee could perform the job or that he was purposely failing. In order to address the problem, she had to develop written standards, retrain the employee, and give him a fair chance to succeed. In this case, when she began to coach and train the employee, his performance improved and a termination was not necessary.

Take a Moment

Supervisors often have a difficult time demonstrating performance standards. Look around your work unit. If you were asked to document performance standards, how would you do it? Do you have production manuals, employee-training records, memos, or other documentation that could be used to demonstrate that you've communicated performance standards to your employees?

Termination Without a Valid, Objective Reason

An employer who fires an employee without a valid, objective reason can expect to be exposed to the outrage of judges and juries. Few, if any, juries will accept that an employee may be fired without a valid, objective reason.

One of the worst legal cases in the wrongful discharge area started because an employer told a senior vice president that he was fired and that he should "look in his heart" to find the reason. That case has become a landmark in wrongful discharge litigation. It exposed the company to millions of dollars worth of negative publicity. In addition, that statement cost the company hundreds of thousands of dollars in administrative and legal expenses. The total cost was far more than an objective explanation to the employee at the time of the termination ever would have cost.

5

Subjective Reasons

Subjective opinions usually do not stand up in court cases.

In a court case, a company laid off two employees; one belonged to a minority group. The minority worker was never recalled, even though the white employee was rehired and other Caucasian employees were hired to fill positions. In response to the minority employee's discrimination claim, the company manager stated that the reason the minority employee was not rehired was because she was "not a good employee." Of course, there was nothing in the file to support that allegation.

The court found the company liable on the grounds that the manager's subjective evaluation, "not a good employee," was without objective support and, therefore, not a sufficient defense to a discrimination claim.

Subjective opinions usually do not stand up in court cases. Courts and juries increasingly are rejecting subjective statements such as "poor attitude" or "disruptive" and are requiring objective facts to support employment decisions. Courts are demanding factual, behavioral observations in which the manager describes the exact behavior problems of the employee.

In many cases, supervisors who terminated employees for reasons such as "incompatibility," "disloyalty," and "poor attitude" have faced courts that found their subjective statements were thin disguises for unlawful discrimination.

Subterfuge Reasons

In another court case, a company was thinking about terminating an employee for lack of work (a layoff). At the same time, it was considering a new employee to fill the position as soon as it became vacant. A termination under these circumstances is not a layoff. Rather, it is subterfuge. The company is saying one thing (lack of work) but doing another (hiring someone else to do the work).

Periodically, companies will try to lay off employees instead of firing them. Sometimes the real reason is illegal discrimination. More often, though, the manager simply does not want to take time to do the necessary documentation and confront the employee with the true issues. In other words, the manager is looking for a fast, easy way to fire the employee. Regardless of the reason, a subterfuge termination is one of the fastest ways for a company to incur a substantial legal penalty.

In still another case, an employee was terminated and told that it was a layoff due to lack of work. When other employees were recalled, the company refused to take the employee back. The employee filed a discrimination charge against the company and the manager. At the hearing, the manager stated that the employee was incompetent but that, to be nice to him, he had told him he was being laid off. The EEOC agent looked at the manager and said, "Well, we've established that you tell lies. What we don't know is how often."

If the company does not give the employee the real reason he or she is being disciplined, it probably means that management has not done its job documenting the employee's behavior. If the employee cannot be told the real reason, the company should seriously consider whether the manager—not the employee—should be disciplined. Firing an employee and lying about the reason is just another form of legal roulette; sooner or later, the company will pay.

5

Historic Reasons

In some cases in which an employee has performed poorly or has violated a serious company rule, the manager may decide not to terminate the employee. Instead, the manager will give him or her a last chance to improve. The employee then may make an effort and reach the minimum performance standards for the job. In frustration, the manager finally decides to discharge the employee and recommends his or her dismissal.

In fact, what is happening in cases like this is that, despite the employee's efforts, the manager has lost confidence in him or her. The manager wants to go back in history and use old performance issues to terminate the employee. In many cases, those issues will be too old to be used; if they are used, it can appear that the manager is out to get the employee.

When a supervisor makes a decision to give an employee a chance, it is not a chance to fail but a chance to succeed. If the employee does succeed on the job, the manager must forget the loss of confidence and keep the employee.

After-the-Fact Reasons

If additional reasons for discipline are discovered after an employee has been terminated and the company expects litigation, the company must conduct an investigation just as if the employee still were employed. If the investigation reveals legitimate reasons for a termination, the company should terminate the employee a second time. Some cases have been dropped and litigation ended after an employee received a second termination notice explaining that additional facts were discovered after the employee was terminated, and that these facts constitute separate, sufficient grounds for termination.

Negotiated Resignation

In some cases, it is better to negotiate for an employee's resignation than it is to pursue termination. In these cases, the employee frequently receives some sort of cash settlement in exchange for leaving the company and signing a written release that frees the company of any legal liability. You never should enter into such an agreement without the advice and counsel of a competent labor attorney. In a number of cases, courts have held that if an employee freely agrees to resign and give up any lawsuit against an employer in exchange for some new consideration from the company, the resignation is binding and the employee cannot sue.

Periodically a company will encounter a situation in which it wants to terminate an employee when there is no valid, objective reason for termination. An example is the employee who had worked at a company for 15 years. Although his sales had steadily declined, he never had been given a performance objective or a performance review. The company needed to make a turnaround in the department, but it would have taken months to document the employee. Instead his resignation was negotiated.

5

Self-Check: Chapter 5 Review

Now that you've read Chapter 5, use this space to review what you've learned. If you aren't sure of an answer, just refer to the text. Suggested answers appear on page 85.

1. Why is it important to use progressive discipline?

   _____

   _____

   _____

2. The progressive discipline steps above the Consequence Line are _____ steps. The progressive discipline steps below the Consequence Line are _____ steps.

3. What are the three objective reasons for terminating an employee?

   a._____

   b._____

   c._____

4. What is a subterfuge termination?

    _____

    _____

    _____

    _____

5. When a company negotiates a resignation with an employee, it needs to: (Circle one)

    a. Consult a labor attorney for advice.

    b. Be sure the employee understands his or her rights.

    c. Put the agreement between the company and the employee in writing.

    d. All of the above.

5

Chapter *Six*

Meeting with the Employee

Chapter Objectives

▶ Plan a meeting to ask an employee to explain his or her side of an issue that concerns you.

▶ Plan a meeting with an employee to discuss a performance or rule-violation issue.

▶ Use the FOSA+ system as an agenda to successfully conduct a meeting that helps an employee understand the future performance you expect.

Discipline-Related Meetings

There are two types of meetings you'll need to conduct when you address employee discipline:

There are two types of meetings you'll need to conduct when you address employee discipline.

◆ *The information-gathering meeting,* in which you collect information from the employee or from witnesses

◆ *The disciplinary meeting,* in which you explain a disciplinary action to an employee

Your approach to and handling of this type of meeting will determine whether the employee responds to your disciplinary action in a positive or negative manner.

Meeting with an Employee and Witnesses

Before you decide to take any disciplinary action, be sure your information is accurate. In our highly litigious society, an employee could likely challenge your decision to discipline or terminate him or her. When that happens, you will need to be able to demonstrate that your decision was fair and reasonable.

One way to ensure that your information is accurate is to interview the employee and any witnesses. Your interviews must be designed to determine exactly what happened (the facts), not to prove that the employee was wrong.

It is especially important that you talk to the employee to hear his or her side of the story. If you do not take the time to hold this meeting, the employee very likely will feel that you dealt with him or her unfairly. No one likes to be the subject of disciplinary action, but it is almost impossible to accept if you feel it was taken without regard for your perspective.

Before you decide to take any disciplinary action, be sure your information is accurate.

Preparing for Your Meetings

You should never attempt to meet with an employee or a witness to collect information unless you are thoroughly prepared. To prepare for the meeting, you first must review all of the information you already have—information such as:

◆ Witness statements

◆ Personnel files

◆ Your incidents diary

◆ Current and past company policies

◆ Current and past company practices

◆ Union contracts

◆ Other related information

6

Before you hold a meeting, check with your human resources representative and/or legal counsel. These labor relations experts should help you plan for the meeting. They also will advise you whether the employee is entitled to have a representative present at the meeting.

> **As you plan for your meeting or meetings, it's a good idea to ask another manager to be present in the room with you.**

When you meet with an employee or a witness to collect information, you might not get everything you feel you need to make your decision. You may have to hold a second round of meetings to clarify issues or ask for new information.

As part of your preparation, ask another manager to be present in the room with you during the meeting or meetings. The role of this manager is to listen carefully to the discussion and to take notes. We call this person a *silent witness*.

Conducting Your Meetings

Begin each session by explaining that the reason you called the meeting is to collect information. Tell the employee about the situation that has you concerned, and ask what he or she knows about the issues.

The Importance of Listening

Listen carefully to what you hear. In most cases, you'll want to listen to the entire explanation without taking notes so you don't miss anything that's said. (Remember, your silent witness will be taking notes.) Once the employee or witness completes his or her explanation, ask the person to go back to the beginning and tell you everything again, this time taking notes and asking questions to clarify the information you're getting. After you've heard the story a second time, read your notes to the employee or witness and ask him or her if you've gotten the story correctly. You might even ask the employee or witness to read your notes and initial them. At this point, you also may want to ask the employee or witness to write out his or her story.

Objectively Analyzing the Information

When you complete your investigation, ask a third party to objectively analyze the information you've collected. Conduct your third-party review with the help of a senior manager and/or human resources or legal counsel.

The third-party review has three purposes:

1. **To ensure that your information is complete.** Before you take any disciplinary action, you must be sure that you have a complete and accurate picture of the issues you're addressing.

2. **To ensure that you're proceeding in a fair and objective manner.** Remember the plus in the FOSA+ system. It is a reminder that your actions need to create an opportunity for the employee to succeed. Your manager, human resources representative, or legal counsel will be able to review your case and make sure your actions are fair and equitable.

3. **To give you an opportunity to compare your proposed disciplinary action to the actions of other company supervisors in similar cases.** The same rules and performance standards must apply to all employees. If you discipline an employee when another supervisor has ignored similar behavior, you may be setting yourself up for a discrimination claim.

6

Take a Moment

Who in your company is responsible for helping you review disciplinary actions? What kinds of information and documentation do they expect you to provide? How often do you and other supervisors meet with this person to discuss employee relations practices in your company?

The Discipline Meeting

If you decide to take a formal disciplinary action, it's time to write your FOSA+ letter. Double-check your letter to make sure your facts are accurate and complete and that the letter is error-free.

When you meet with the employee, focus on the plus in the FOSA+ system. Explain the situation and why it is a problem to you and the company. Your goal here is not to assess blame but to help the employee understand why the issues are issues and why they affect him or her. If you explain the problem clearly with facts, the employee likely will be more receptive to your points and will consider what he or she needs to do to resolve the problem. Let the employee ask questions, and do not argue about the facts. But if the employee points out something you did not know or raises a doubt in your mind about the accuracy of your facts, you should put your disciplinary action on hold and continue your investigation.

After you explain the problem and after you feel the employee understands why it is a problem, move the discussion to objectives. Start by asking the employee for his or her ideas about how to resolve the problem and meet your objectives. Many times, those solutions will match your own. If they do, the employee will be much more likely to accept your objectives and work toward them. But if they do not, you will need to offer your own solutions, which will demonstrate that your goal is to create an opportunity for the employee to succeed. Even though your solutions are suggestions and not requirements, make sure the employee knows that meeting or exceeding your objectives—through whatever solutions—is a requirement.

Take a Moment

When you meet with an employee or witness, select a meeting place that is comfortable and free of distractions. Here is a checklist of points to consider.

- Does the room you plan to use have a reasonably private entrance so the employee or witness isn't subject to undue attention when he or she enters?

- Are the windows covered and closed so that others can't look in or overhear the conversation?

- Is the room free of unnecessary distractions, such as pictures, unrelated paperwork, or other materials?

- Is there a comfortable chair for each participant and a writing surface to help you take notes?

- Is there a place outside the room for the employee or witness to securely leave personal property that doesn't need to be in the meeting room?

6

Final Steps of the Discipline Meeting

Finally, explain to the employee that you are disciplining him or her and that if the employee does not meet or exceed the objectives you've established, he or she will be subject to further disciplinary action, up to and including termination.

When you give the employee the written discipline notice, also ask him or her to sign it to acknowledge receiving a copy. If the employee refuses to sign the memo, note the refusal on the memo, date your note, and give a copy of the memo to the employee. (In most cases, you should ask the witness to initial the memo to indicate that the employee refused to sign.) Place the original copy of the memo in the employee's personnel file.

Follow-Up

After you give the employee the discipline notice, it's important to follow up with him or her in the near future.

After you give the employee the discipline notice, it's important to follow up with him or her in the near future. Mark your calendar to remind you to follow up. Part of being a good coach (the plus in the FOSA+ system) is working with the person after you talk to him or her. If the employee is doing well, say so. But if the employee is continuing to have problems, communicate that, too, and, if appropriate, take additional disciplinary action.

Self-Check: Chapter 6 Review

Now that you've read Chapter 6, use this space to review what you've learned. If you aren't sure of an answer, just refer to the text. Suggested answers appear on pages 85 and 86.

1. What are the two types of meetings you need to conduct when you take a disciplinary action?

    a._____

    b._____

2. Why is it important to give an employee the opportunity to explain his or her story before you take a disciplinary action?

    _____

    _____

3. What are the three reasons for asking an objective third party to review your investigation before you take a disciplinary action?

    a._____

    b._____

    c._____

4. How can you use the FOSA+ system in your meeting with the employee?

    _____

5. Why is it important to follow up with an employee after you take a disciplinary action?

    _____

    _____

6

Suggested Answers to Exercises

Chapter One

1. a. Outline a disciplinary-action memo.
   b. Plan an agenda for meeting with an employee.

2. a. To provide a record of actions being taken by the organization that can be used as a legal defense.
   b. To help the employee understand his or her supervisor's concerns and what to do about them.
   c. To help a supervisor be more objective and fair before taking a disciplinary action.
   d. To help ensure that all supervisors are consistent in dealing with employee problems.

3. To train (a person) to act according to the expected norm.

4. a. Trainers
   b. Coaches

5. a. Investigate to be sure you have a complete and accurate explanation of the employee's behavior.
   b. Review the situation with your senior manager or a human resources representative before deciding what action, if any, to take.

Chapter Two

1. c. To keep track of incidents as they occur so positive and critical employee documentation are factual and accurate.

2. False—You should talk to an employee about the issues you note in your incidents diary.

3. The best place to keep an incidents diary is where you'll have easy and regular access to it. It should be accessible only to you. For most supervisors, a calendar is the best place to keep an incidents diary.

4. You should keep notes about positive performance, performance objectives, investigations, counseling and coaching, progressive discipline, and other information related to performance and rule violations.

Chapter Three

1. Facts describe the situation or issue without emotion. They are objective, not subjective. Facts allow the employee to draw his or her own conclusions about the situation you are describing.

2. For example:
   I walked into the lobby at 10:00 a.m. and saw you pick up the phone. I heard you say, "Yo dude. Thanks for calling Kids Motorhomes. Who do you want to be jiving with this morning?" When I asked you why you had answered the phone that way . . . .

3. False—It's important to have the witness sign a statement to confirm that he or she actually provided the information.

4. b. They provide a more complete explanation of why you are taking a particular action.

Chapter Four

1. a. Give the employee a specific behavior pattern to follow,
    b. Set a specific result for the employee to achieve.

2. a. Specific
    b. Positive
    c. Required
    d. Complete

3. For example:
    Hotel Front-Desk Clerk
    In the future, you must complete your paperwork before the end of your shift. By complete, I mean that you must alphabetize and file all of the registration slips for guests who registered at your station during your shift. You must make notes in the shift log about any problems or guest complaints that come to your attention during your shift. You must log off of your computer before you leave your work station at the end of the shift.

4. A solution shows that the supervisor offered to coach the employee and made an attempt to help him or her succeed.

5. The statement is an objective because it tells the employee that he or she must greet customers in a certain way.

6. An action communicates the seriousness of the situation and your commitment to seeing the employee resolve the problem. It also communicates to the employee that his or her job is in jeopardy.

7. b. Employees, the law, and the courts look to supervisors to provide leadership. Good leaders set the example and work to help their people understand their roles and responsibilities.

Chapter Five

1. Progressive discipline demonstrates that you have made a reasonable effort to create an opportunity to help an employee succeed.

2. The progressive discipline steps above the Consequence Line are *formal* steps. The progressive discipline steps below the Consequence Line are *informal* steps.

3. a. Reduction in force
   b. Violation of company rules
   c. Inability or failure to perform

4. A *subterfuge termination* occurs when an employee is given a reason for the termination that is not the true reason.

5. d. All of the above.

Chapter Six

1. a. Information-gathering meetings
   b. Disciplinary meetings

2. Most people consider it a basic right to explain what they know about a situation before a manager takes an action against them. Meeting with the employee before you make a decision sends a message that you are trying to be fair and objective.

3. a. To ensure that you have complete information before you take an action.
   b. To ensure that your action is fair and objective.
   c. To ensure that your action is consistent with those of other supervisors.

4. The FOSA+ system can serve as an agenda for a meeting with an employee. When it is followed, it provides an objective guideline for the discussion between the supervisor and the employee to ensure that the employee understands the problem and what he or she needs to do to resolve it.

5. First, follow-up reinforces the importance of the issue. Second, it gives you an opportunity to reinforce positive behavior. And third, it helps you take timely action if the employee is not responding to the original discipline.